David & C
Cross Stitch Co...

A DAVID & CHARLES BOOK

First published in the UK in 2004

Designs copyright © Joan Elliott,
Sam Hawkins, Brenda Keyes,
Gillian Souter 2004
Text, layout, photographs copyright
© David & Charles 2004

Distributed in North America
by F&W Publications, Inc.
4700 East Galbraith Road
Cincinnati, OH 45236
1-800-289-0963

Joan Elliott, Sam Hawkins, Brenda
Keyes and Gillian Souter have
asserted their right to be identified
as authors of this work in
accordance with the Copyright,
Designs and Patents Act, 1988.

A catalogue record for this book is
available from the British Library.

ISBN 0 7153 1757 1

Printed in Singapore by KHL
for David & Charles
Brunel House Newton Abbot Devon

Visit our website at
www.davidandcharles.co.uk

David & Charles books are
available from all good bookshops;
alternatively you can contact our
Orderline on (0)1626 334555
or write to us at FREEPOST
EX2110, David & Charles Direct,
Newton Abbot, TQ12 4ZZ (no
stamp required UK mainland).

Christmas Stockings

Contents

Noel's Christmas Stocking
© Gillian Souter

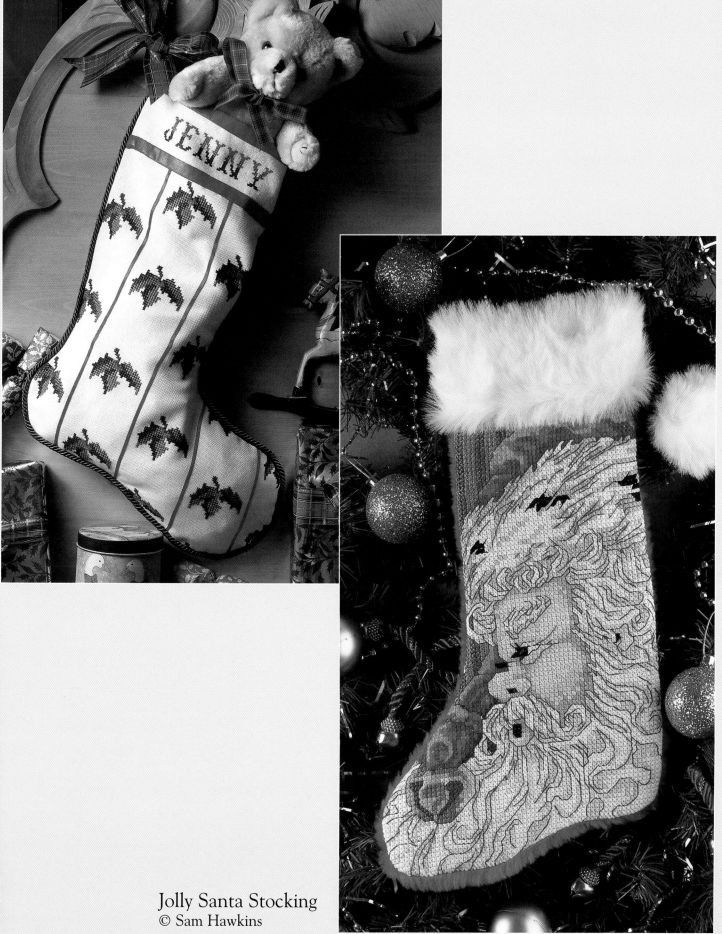

Holly Stocking
© Brenda Keyes

Jolly Santa Stocking
© Sam Hawkins

3

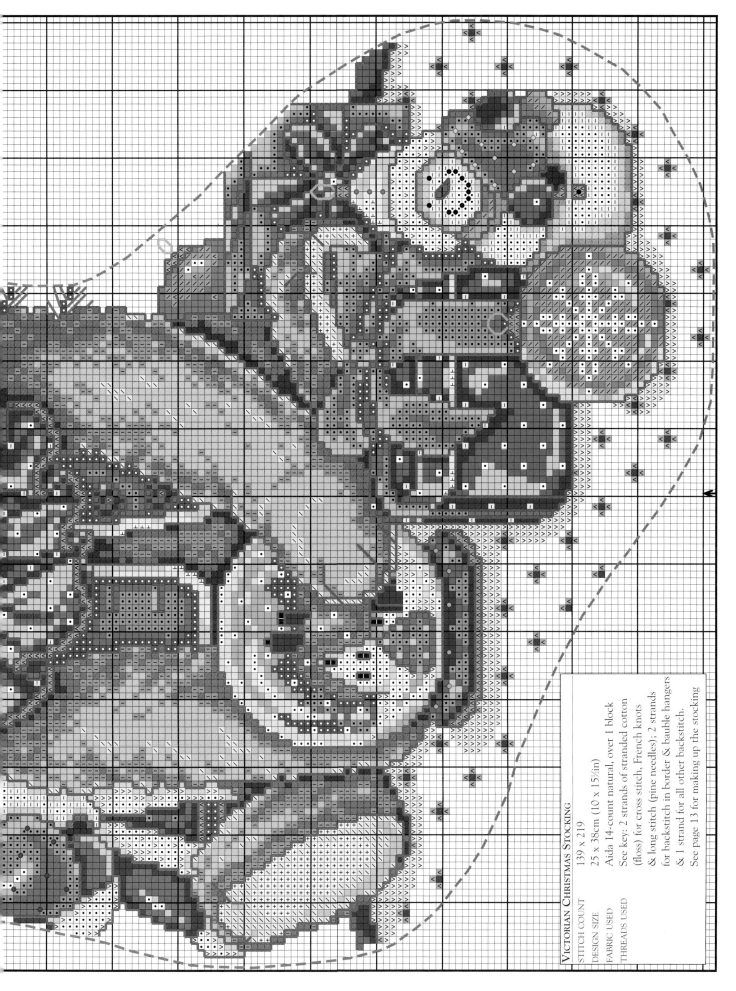

VICTORIAN CHRISTMAS STOCKING

STITCH COUNT   139 x 219

DESIGN SIZE   25 x 38cm (10 x 15¼in)

FABRIC USED   Aida 14-count natural, over 1 block

THREADS USED   See key: 2 strands of stranded cotton
(floss) for cross stitch, French knots
& long stitch (pine needles); 2 strands
for backstitch in border & bauble hangers
& 1 strand for all other backstitch.
See page 13 for making up the stocking

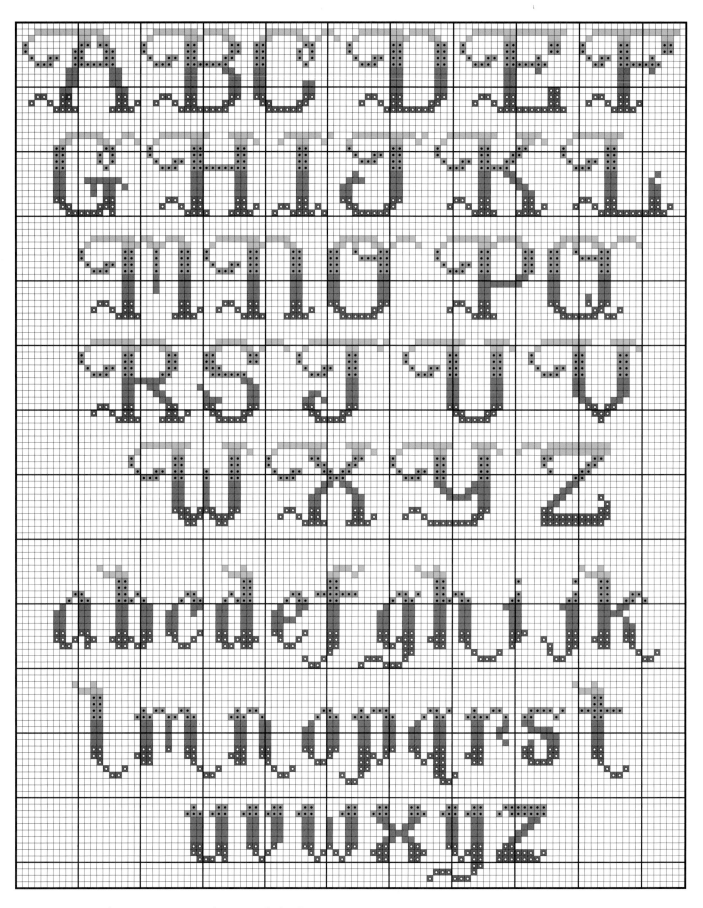

Victorian Christmas Stocking Alphabet

DMC STRANDED COTTON

- 700
- 704
- • 702
- ◉ 3818

Noel's Christmas Stocking

DMC STRANDED COTTON

Cross stitch		Backstitch	
■	310	◩	310
■	321	◩	415
■	415	◩	444
■	444	◩	721
■	721	◩	white
·	white	**French knots**	
		●	310

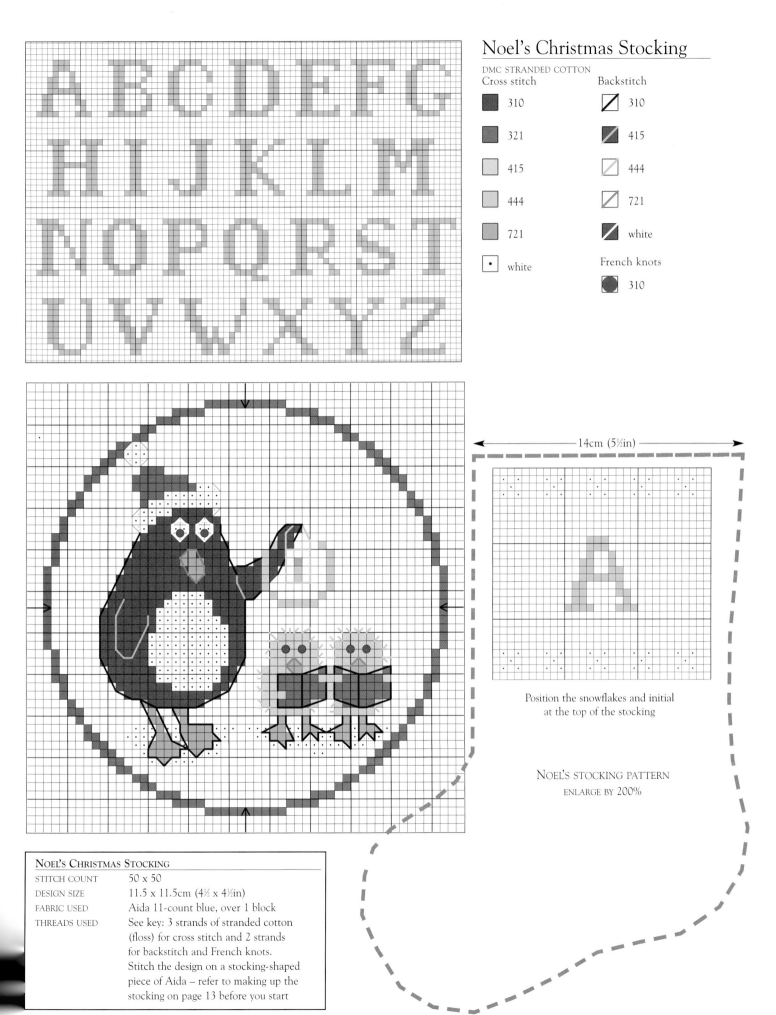

14cm (5½in)

Position the snowflakes and initial
at the top of the stocking

NOEL'S STOCKING PATTERN
ENLARGE BY 200%

NOEL'S CHRISTMAS STOCKING	
STITCH COUNT	50 x 50
DESIGN SIZE	11.5 x 11.5cm (4½ x 4½in)
FABRIC USED	Aida 11-count blue, over 1 block
THREADS USED	See key: 3 strands of stranded cotton (floss) for cross stitch and 2 strands for backstitch and French knots. Stitch the design on a stocking-shaped piece of Aida – refer to making up the stocking on page 13 before you start

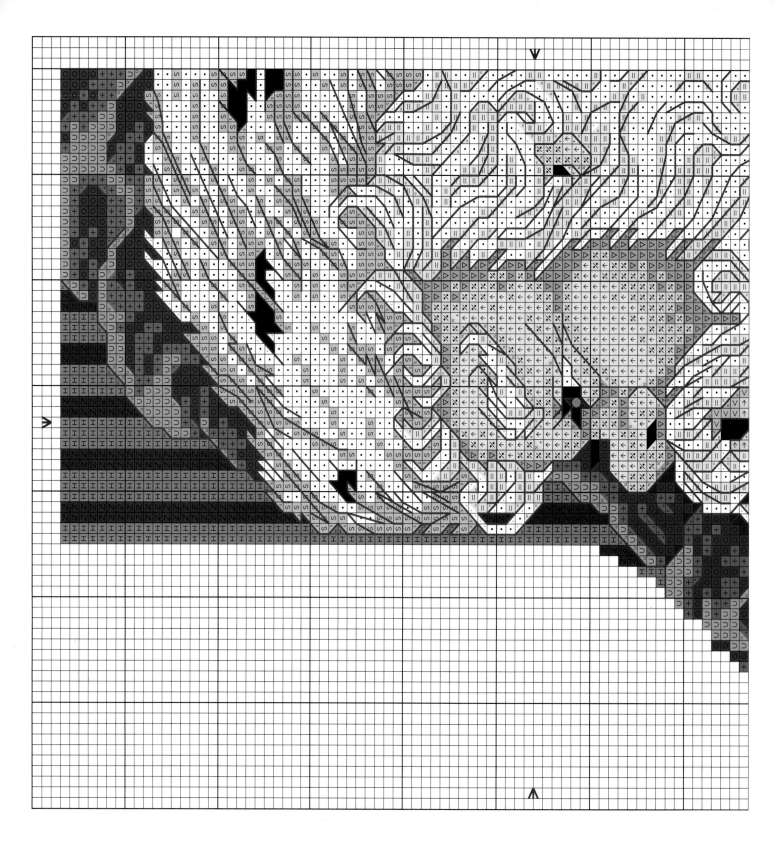

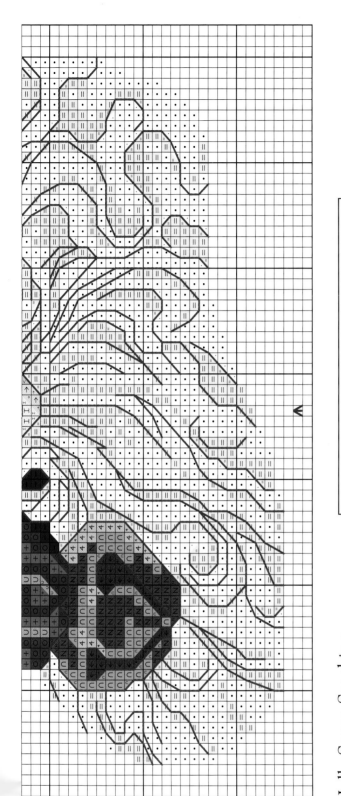

Jolly Santa Stocking

JOLLY SANTA STOCKING	
STITCH COUNT	67 x 102
DESIGN SIZE	21.2 x 32.3cm (8⅜ x 12¾in)
FABRIC USED	Evenweave 32-count cream Belfast linen, over 4 fabric threads
THREADS USED	See key: 5 strands of stranded cotton (floss) for cross stitch and 2 for backstitch. See page 13 for making up the stocking

DMC STRANDED COTTON

Cross stitch

·	blanc	↑	776	=	3753
■	310	∩	783	▷	3773
+	321	↓	801		Backstitch
N	434	O	815	╱	310
N	561	I	818	╱	801
H	562	U	893		French knots
+	725	V	899	●	310
S	738	▌	902		
%	754	←	948		

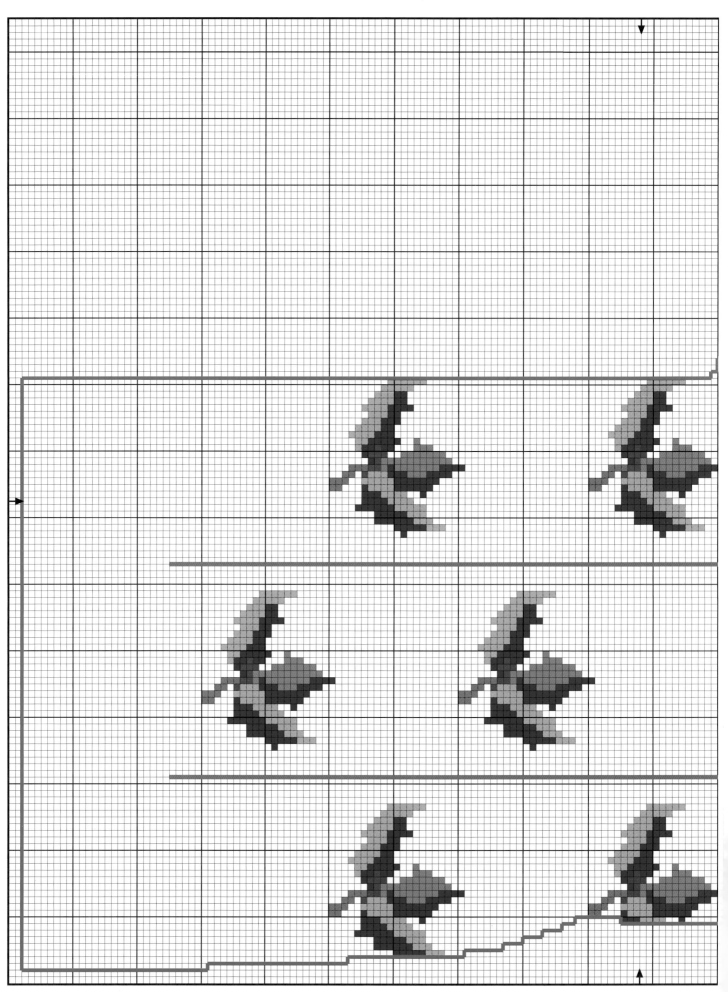

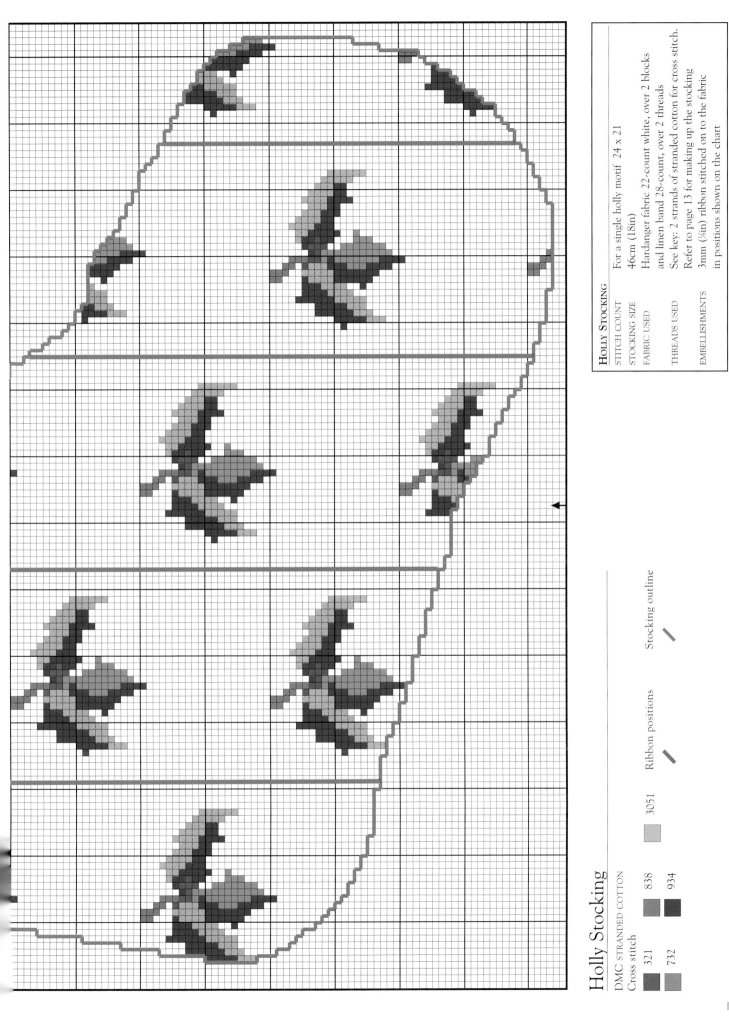

Holly Stocking

DMC STRANDED COTTON
Cross stitch

321	838
732	934
	3051

Ribbon positions

Stocking outline

HOLLY STOCKING

STITCH COUNT	For a single holly motif 24 x 21
STOCKING SIZE	46cm (18in)
FABRIC USED	Hardanger fabric 22-count white, over 2 blocks and linen band 28-count, over 2 threads
THREADS USED	See key: 2 strands of stranded cotton for cross stitch.
EMBELLISHMENTS	Refer to page 13 for making up the stocking 3mm (⅛in) ribbon stitched on to the fabric in positions shown on the chart

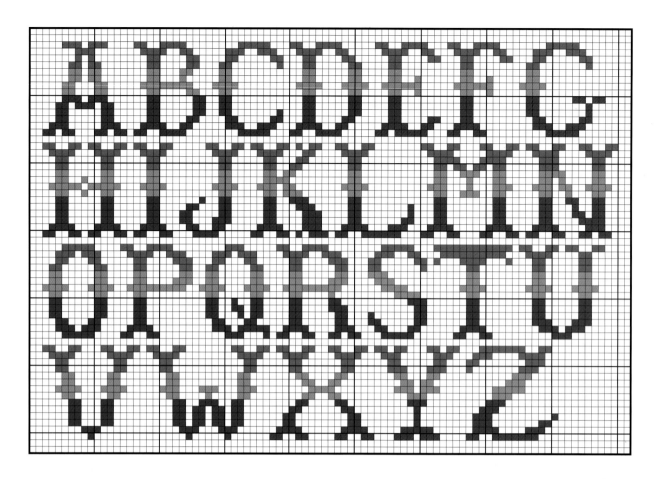

Holly Stocking Alphabet

DMC STRANDED COTTON
Cross stitch

321

732

934

Making Up the Stockings

VICTORIAN CHRISTMAS STOCKING

You will need: fusible fleece, backing/lining fabric, decorative braid and matching sewing thread. (See photo page 2.)

1 Once the embroidery is complete use a contrasting thread to tack (baste) a stocking outline all round the design edges, 1.25cm (½in) out from the red dotted line shown on the chart. Place fusible fleece on the wrong side of the stocking, covering all of the tacking (basting) stitches and with an additional 1.25cm (½in) at the top. Press to fuse according to the manufacturer's directions. Turn the stocking over and cut the top edge seven rows above the tacked line, then cut the remaining stocking shape along the tacked (basted) lines. Fold the top edge to the wrong side along the tacked line and press.

2 Cut the backing/lining fabric into two pieces 56 x 46cm (22 x 18in) and with right sides together place under the stocking and cut to the stocking shape, adding an extra 10cm (4in) at the top. Layer the fabric and stocking as follows: one piece of fabric right side up, the stocking right side up, and the second piece of fabric wrong side up (see diagram below). Pin together and stitch a 1.25cm (½in) seam all round leaving the top edge open and a small gap at the bottom for tucking in the decorative braid later. Finish off the raw edges by folding over 1.25cm (½in) to the wrong side and stitching down. Turn the embroidery to the outside, creating a lining and backing. Fold the two top flaps in, aligning them with the folded edge of the embroidery.

3 Make a hanging loop from 20cm (8in) of decorative braid. Fold in half and tuck the ends into the left corner of the top edge, between the embroidery and lining. Slipstitch the lining and embroidery together at the top edge, catching the cord securely. Attach more braid to the edge of the stocking, slipstitching all round the stocking and tucking the ends into the opening in the bottom seam. Slipstitch this seam closed.

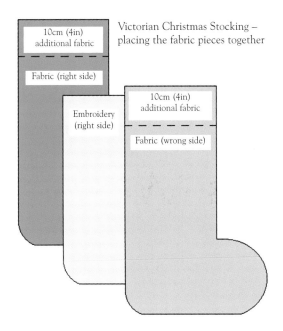

Victorian Christmas Stocking – placing the fabric pieces together

10cm (4in) additional fabric

Fabric (right side)

10cm (4in) additional fabric

Embroidery (right side)

Fabric (wrong side)

NOEL'S CHRISTMAS STOCKING

You will need: lining fabric, bias binding and matching sewing thread. (See photo page 2.)

1 Enlarge the stocking pattern on page 7 on a photocopier by 200%. Cut out the shape and use it as a template to mark the pattern on two pieces of Aida fabric. Stitch the Noel design in the lower part of one of the pieces and two rows of snowflakes along the top, 4.5cm (1¾in) apart – see diagram on page 7. Cross stitch a child's name between the snowflakes if you wish, using the alphabet on page 7.

2 Make up the stocking by cutting two pieces of lining fabric 25 x 35cm (10 x 13in). Place the embroidered Aida on a piece of lining fabric, right sides together, and sew a 1.25cm (½in) seam across the top edge. Turn the right way out and tack (baste) the fabrics together along the raw edge, then trim the lining to the same shape as the Aida fabric. Line the other piece of Aida in the same way.

3 Tack (baste) the front and back of the stocking together. Finish raw edges with bias binding and form a hanging loop at the top right corner.

JOLLY SANTA STOCKING

You will need: red fur fabric, white fur fabric, small amount of polyester stuffing, red pyjama cord and matching sewing thread. (See photo page 2.)

1 Once the Santa design has been stitched, cut carefully around the shape, leaving 1.25cm (½in) of blank fabric around the edges. Lay this stocking shape on the reverse side of the red fur fabric, draw around the shape and cut out. With right sides together, pin, tack (baste) and stitch the embroidery and fur fabric together, rounding off sharp corners and clipping seams on the curves.

2 Cut a piece of white fur fabric 15cm (6in) wide and long enough to fit around the top of the stocking, plus 2cm (¾in) for seam allowances. Join the short edges of the white fur cuff with a 1cm (⅜in) seam. With right sides together and working on the wrong side of the stitching, join the cuff to the stocking top, along the top edge of the design. Fold the cuff over to meet the inside of the stocking and attach with small stitches. Turn the stocking to the right side.

3 Make a bobble from a 10cm (4in) circle of white fur. Stitch a row of running stitches around the edge. Place stuffing in the middle and draw up the running stitches. Attach a length of pyjama cord to the bobble and the other end to the stocking cuff on the back seam, allowing enough cord for the bobble to hang below the cuff.

HOLLY STOCKING

You will need: 28-count linen band, red chintz, white lining fabric, narrow ribbon, decorative cord and matching sewing thread. (See photo page 2.)

1 Tack (baste) the stocking outline as shown on the chart on pages 10 and 11 on to a piece of Hardanger fabric and then stitch the design. Stitch the narrow ribbon into place, as shown on the chart, and trim excess fabric to within 1.25cm (½in) of the tacking (basting).

2 Plan your name (see page 15) and stitch it on the 28-count linen band over two threads from the centre out, using the alphabet on page 12.

3 Cut a strip of red chintz 2.5 x 20cm (1 x 8in) and with wrong sides together, fold long sides to middle and tack (baste). Pin, tack (baste) and stitch this strip 1.25cm (½in) away from the bottom edge of the embroidered linen band (see photograph opposite). With wrong sides facing, pin tack (baste) and stitch the band and its chintz edging to the top edge of the embroidered stocking.

4 Pin the stocking shape, wrong sides together, on to red cotton chintz backing fabric and cut the chintz to match. Cut two stocking shapes from white lining fabric. Place the embroidered stocking front and red chintz backing right sides together, then pin, tack (baste) and stitch together 1.25cm (½in) from the edge. Trim excess fabric then turn the right way and iron the seam flat. Sew decorative cord on to the seam.

5 Stitch the two white pieces of fabric together and trim excess. Do not turn inside out. Fit the lining inside the stocking and tack (baste) the top edges together. Now pin and tack (baste) the long red chintz strip right sides together with the top of the stocking. Fold the short ends back on themselves so they just meet and stitch 6mm (¼in) away from the edge. Make a 6mm (¼in) turning on the opposite edge of this binding strip, wrong sides facing and fold over the top of the stocking, concealing raw edges. Stitch into place using small hem stitches.

6 Make a hanging loop using a 17.8 x 6.4cm (7 x 2½in) piece of chintz folded in half lengthways, right sides together. Stitch together along two sides, turn through and close the opening with small stitches. Press flat and stitch firmly in place across the top left corner of the stocking.

Stitching Advice

The following section is relevant throughout the David & Charles *Cross Stitch Collection* series, not just the charts in this book. It will provide you with all the information you need to stitch the designs charted.

MATERIALS

FABRICS

Fabrics used for counted cross stitch are woven so they have the same number of threads or blocks to 2.5cm (1in), both horizontally and vertically. The two main fabric types used are blockweaves such as Aida, and even-weaves such as linen. Cross stitch can also be worked on other fabrics such as waste canvas, plastic canvas and stitching (perforated) paper.

AIDAS These fabrics are woven in blocks and are available in many colours and counts – 8, 11, 14, 16, 18 and 20 blocks to 2.5cm (1in). They are made from various fibres and as different width bands. When stitching on Aida, one block on the fabric corresponds to one square on a chart and each cross stitch is worked over one block.

EVENWEAVES These fabrics are woven singly and are made from various fibres and as different width bands. They are also available in many different colours and counts. When stitching on evenweave, each cross stitch is usually worked over two threads of the fabric.

WASTE CANVAS This is designed for stitching on fabrics where cross stitching wouldn't normally be possible because the threads are uneven, such as clothing. To use, tack (baste) a piece of waste canvas large enough for the design into position on to the chosen article and cross stitch the design through both fabrics. When all stitching is complete, dampen the canvas and use tweezers to draw out the threads. You may find it easier to work backstitches after the canvas has been removed.

PLASTIC CANVAS This is a rigid but flexible mesh-like material that can be cut and assembled into three-dimensional objects. It is available in various counts and as pre-cut shapes. Cross stitches are worked over intersections of the mesh.

STITCHING PAPER Cross stitch designs can be worked on perforated paper which can then be cut, folded and glued to make a variety of items such as cards, bookmarks and notebook covers. The right side is the smoother side of the paper and cross stitch is normally worked with three strands of stranded cotton (floss) and backstitch with two.

THREADS

The most commonly used thread for counted embroidery is stranded cotton (floss) but there are many other types available, including rayons, space-dyed or variegated threads, perlé cottons and metallic threads.

STRANDED COTTON (FLOSS) This six-stranded thread can be bought by the skein in hundreds of colours with ranges made by DMC, Anchor and Madeira (see DMC/Anchor conversion chart at the front of this book). Colours can be mixed or 'tweeded' in the needle. The stitching information with the charts will tell you how many strands to use for a design.

VARIEGATED THREADS There are many lovely variegated threads available now. The chart keys give the name and code of the thread used. When stitching with variegated threads work cross stitches as complete stitches, not in two journeys or the colour sequence will be spoiled.

METALLICS AND BLENDING FILAMENTS Metallic threads are available in many gorgeous colours and finishes from various companies and they can be used in cross stitch designs to create glitter and interest. Blending filaments can be stitched with stranded cotton (floss) to create an over-all sparkle to a design. Use shorter lengths of thread when working with metallics to avoid tangles and excessive wear on the thread.

TAPESTRY WOOL (YARN) Many cross stitch designs can be stitched on canvas in tapestry wool (yarn) instead of stranded cotton (floss), using half cross stitch or tent stitch instead of cross stitch. Ask at needlework shops for suppliers and colour conversions from stranded cotton (floss).

EQUIPMENT

Very little equipment is needed for cross stitch embroidery and the following basics are all you need to get you started.

NEEDLES Use blunt tapestry needles for counted cross stitch. The commonest sizes used are 24 and 26 but the size depends on your project and personal preference. Avoid leaving a needle in the fabric unless it is gold plated or it may cause marks. A beading needle (or fine 'sharp' needle), which is much thinner, will be needed to attach beads.

SCISSORS Use dressmaker's shears for cutting fabric and a small, sharp pair of pointed scissors for cutting embroidery threads.

FRAMES AND HOOPS These are not essential but if you use one, choose one large enough to hold the complete design, to avoid marking the fabric and flattening stitches.

TECHNIQUES

USING CHARTS

The designs in this series are worked from black and white charts with symbols, or colour charts with a black and/or white symbol to aid colour identification. Each square, both occupied and unoccupied, represents one block of Aida or two threads of linen, unless stated otherwise. Each occupied square equals one cross stitch. Some charts also have three-quarter cross stitches (sometimes called fractional stitches) and these usually occupy part of a square, either a triangle or a small square. French knots are indicated by circles, usually coloured in the colour charts and labelled in the key or on the chart. Backstitch (and some-times long stitch) is shown on charts by straight lines, usually coloured in the colour charts, with the code either on the chart or in the key. Arrows at the sides of the charts allow you to find the centre easily.

CALCULATING DESIGN SIZE

Each project gives the stitch count and finished design size but if you plan to work the design on a different count you will need to be able to calculate the finished size. To do this, count the number of stitches in the design and divide this by the fabric count number, e.g., 140 stitches x 140 stitches ÷ by 14-count = a design size of 10 x 10in (25.4 x 25.4cm). Remember that working on evenweave usually means working over two threads not one, so divide the fabric count by 2 before you start. See the bottom of page 15 for a quick stitch count table.

PREPARING FABRICS

The sizes given with the charts are for the finished design size only, therefore you will need to add about 10–12.5cm (4–5in) to both measurements when cutting embroidery fabric, to allow enough fabric around the edges for working and for making up later.

Before you begin stitching, press your embroidery fabric if necessary and trim the selvage or any rough edges. Work from the middle of the fabric and middle of the chart where possible to ensure your design is centred on the fabric. Find the middle of the fabric by folding it in four and pressing lightly. Mark the folds with tailor's chalk or with lines of tacking (basting) following a fabric thread. When working with linen, prepare as described above but also sew a narrow hem around all raw edges to preserve them for finishing later.

STARTING AND FINISHING STITCHING

Unless indicated otherwise, begin stitching in the middle of a design to ensure an adequate margin for making up. Start and finish stitching neatly, avoiding knots which create a lumps.

KNOTLESS LOOP START This start can be used with an even number of strands i.e., 2, 4 or 6. To stitch with two strands, begin with one strand about 80cm (30in). Double the thread and thread the needle with the two ends. Put the needle up through the fabric from the wrong side, where you intend to begin stitching, leaving the loop at the back (see diagram top of page 15). Form a half cross stitch, put the needle back through the fabric and through the waiting loop to anchor the stitch.

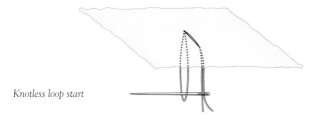

Knotless loop start

AWAY WASTE KNOT START Start this way if using an odd number of strands. Thread the needle with the number of strands required and knot the end. Insert the needle into the right side of the fabric, away from where you wish to begin stitching (see diagram below). Stitch towards the knot and cut it off when the threads are anchored. Alternatively, snip off the knot, thread a needle and work under a few stitches to anchor.

Away waste knot start

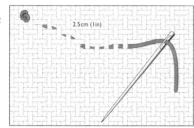

2.5cm (1in)

FINISHING STITCHING At the back of the work, pass the needle and thread under several stitches and snip off the loose end close to the stitching. Begin new colours by passing through stitches on the back in a similar way.

NUMBER OF STRANDS

Stranded cotton (floss) is available in six-stranded skeins and different numbers of strands will be needed for use on different gauges of fabric. Generally two strands are used for cross stitch and one for backstitch but the following table gives further advice.

HOW MANY STRANDS?

FABRIC	NUMBER OF STRANDS OF STRANDED COTTON
6-count Aida	6 or 8 for cross stitch, 2 for backstitch
8-count Aida	6 for cross stitch, 2 for backstitch
11-count Aida & 22-count evenweave (over 2 threads)	3 for cross stitch, 1 for backstitch
14-count Aida & 28-count evenweave (over 2 threads)	2 or 3 for cross stitch, 1 for backstitch
16-count Aida & 32-count evenweave (over 2 threads)	2 for cross stitch, 1 for backstitch
18-count Aida & 36-count evenweave (over 2 threads)	1 or 2 for cross stitch, 1 for backstitch

BLENDING THREADS

Many threads can be used together in the needle to create new colour combinations or to add the shine and glitter of metallic threads such as blending filament. Simply thread the needle with both threads, usually one strand of each, and stitch as normal.

CHANGING NAMES AND DATES

Some cross stitch designs feature names and dates or other wording which you will need to alter using the alphabet provided (or one of your own favourites). Before you begin to stitch, ensure the words will fit the space by counting the squares in the space available (width and height) and marking this on square graph paper. Pencil the letters or numbers on the graph paper, remembering the spaces between letters and words.

ATTACHING BEADS, CHARMS AND BUTTONS

Bead positions are shown on the charts as circles (coloured in the colour charts), with details of the bead type in the key. You might find using a frame or hoop is helpful to keep the fabric taut as you pull the thread firmly to keep the beads in position. Attach beads using a beading needle or very fine 'sharp' needle, thread which matches the bead colour and a half cross stitch (or a full cross stitch if you prefer).

Charm and button positions are usually shown on the chart or described in the key or shown on the photograph of the model. Attach charms and buttons with matching thread.

If you cannot find the beads, charms or buttons suggested on the charts simply substitute something else – there is a wealth to choose from nowadays.

USING RIBBON

Narrow ribbon can be used to create additional interest in a cross stitch design. It may be used to form stitches, such as simple straight stitches, lazy daisy stitch or detached chain stitch. It can also be couched flat on to the fabric and held in place with cross stitches or narrow straight stitches or beads. Ribbon can also be threaded through evenweave fabric after several threads have been removed to create a channel.

TIPS FOR PERFECT STITCHING

● Organize your threads before you start a project as this will help to avoid confusion later. Always include the manufacturer's name and the shade number.

● Separate the strands on a skein of stranded cotton (floss) before taking the number you need to stitch with. Realign them before threading your needle.

● If using a frame, try to avoid a hoop as it will stretch the fabric and leave a mark that may be difficult to remove.

● Plan your route around a chart, counting over short distances wherever possible to avoid mistakes.

● Work your cross stitch in two directions in a sewing movement – half cross stitch in one direction and then cover those original stitches with the second row. This forms single vertical lines on the back that are very neat and give somewhere to finish raw ends. For neat work the top stitches should all face the same direction.

● If adding a backstitch outline, always add it after the cross stitch has been completed to prevent the solid line being broken.

QUICK STITCH COUNTS (see Calculating Design Size, page 14)

FABRIC	STITCH COUNT									
	20	30	40	50	60	70	80	90	100	110
11-count Aida & 22-count evenweave	1¾in (4.6cm)	2¾in (7cm)	3½in (9.2cm)	4½in (11.5cm)	5½in (13.8cm)	6¼in (16cm)	7¼in (18.5cm)	8⅛in (20.7cm)	9in (23cm)	10in (25.4cm)
14-count Aida & 28-count evenweave	1½in (3.6cm)	2⅛in (5.4cm)	2¾in (7.2cm)	3½in (9cm)	4¼in (10.8cm)	5in (12.7cm)	5¾in (14.5cm)	6½in (16.3cm)	7⅛in (18cm)	7⅞in (20cm)
16-count Aida & 32-count evenweave	1¼in (3cm)	1¼in (4.8cm)	2½in (6.3cm)	3⅛in (8cm)	3¾in (9.5cm)	4¼in (11cm)	5in (12.7cm)	5½in (14.3cm)	6¼in (16cm)	6¾in (17.4cm)
18-count Aida & 36-count evenweave	1⅛in (2.8cm)	1½in (4.2cm)	2¼in (5.6cm)	2¾in (7cm)	3⅜in (8.5cm)	3¾in (9.8cm)	4½in (11.3cm)	5in (12.7cm)	5½in (14cm)	6⅛in (15.5cm)

THE STITCHES

ALGERIAN EYE

This star-shaped stitch is a pulled stitch which creates 'holes' in the fabric. It can be worked over two or four threads of evenweave and is more successful on evenweave than Aida.

Start to the left of a vertical thread and work from left to right around each stitch in an anticlockwise direction (or vice versa but keeping each stitch the same). Pass the needle down through the central hole and pull quite firmly so a small hole is formed in the centre. Take care that trailing threads do not cover the hole as you progress.

BACKSTITCH

Backstitch is used for outlining, to add detail or emphasis and for lettering. It is added after the cross stitch to prevent the backstitch line being broken. It is usually indicated on a chart by solid lines with the suggested shade on the chart or key.

Follow the numbered sequence, right, working the stitches over one block of Aida or two threads of evenweave.

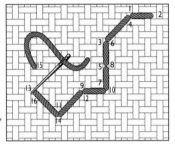

CROSS STITCH

This simple little stitch is the most commonly used stitch in this book. Cross stitches can be worked singly or in two journeys but for neat stitching, keep the top stitch facing the same direction. It does not matter which way it faces but it should be the same for the whole project.

CROSS STITCH ON AIDA

Cross stitch on Aida fabric is normally worked over one block.

To work one complete cross stitch
Follow the numbered sequence in the diagram: bring the needle up through the fabric at the bottom left corner, cross one block of the fabric and insert the needle at the top right corner. Push the needle
through and bring it up at the bottom right corner, ready to complete the stitch in the top left corner. To work the adjacent stitch, bring the needle up at the bottom right-hand corner of the first stitch.

To work cross stitches in two journeys
Work the first leg of the cross stitch as above but instead of completing the stitch, work the adjacent half stitch and continue on to the end of the row. Complete all the crosses by working the other diagonals on the return journey.

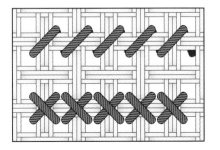

CROSS STITCH ON EVENWEAVE

Cross stitch on evenweave is usually worked over two threads of the fabric in each direction to even out any oddities in the thickness of the fibres. Bring the needle up to the left of a vertical thread, which will make it easier to spot counting mistakes. Work your cross stitch in two directions, as described before. This forms neat, single vertical lines on the back and gives somewhere to finish raw ends.

THREE-QUARTER CROSS STITCH

Three-quarter cross stitch is a fractional stitch which produces the illusion of curves when working cross stitch designs. The stitch can be formed on either Aida or evenweave but is more successful on evenweave. They are usually shown on charts as a triangle (half square).

Work the first half of a cross stitch as usual. Work the second 'quarter' stitch over the top and down into the central hole to anchor the first half of the stitch. If using Aida, you will need to push the needle through the centre of a block of the fabric. Where two three-quarter stitches lie back-to-back in the space of one full cross stitch, work both of the respective 'quarter' stitches into the central hole.

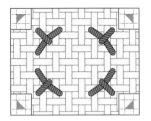

Some designs use half cross stitch and quarter cross stitch and these are, respectively, a single diagonal line and a quarter of a diagonal line.

FRENCH KNOT

French knots are shown on charts as circles, coloured on colour charts. Bring the needle through to the front of the fabric and wind the thread around the needle twice. Put the needle partly through to the back, one thread or part of a block away from the entry point, to stop the stitch being pulled to the wrong side. Gently pull the thread you have wound so that it sits snugly at the point where the needle enters the fabric. Pull the needle through to the back and you should have a perfect knot in position. For bigger knots, add more thread to the needle.

LONG STITCH

This is a long, straight stitch used to create animals' whiskers and so on. Bring the needle and thread up where the stitch is to start and down where the chart indicates it should finish. Occasionally long stitches are couched down – that is, held in place along their length with little stitches, as shown here.

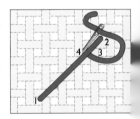

TENT STITCH

This stitch is usually used for working with wool (yarn) on canvas. It looks like half cross stitch from the front but has long, slanting stitches on the back, which
means it uses more yarn and thus is harder wearing. Follow the diagram, taking the needle under the stitches from right to left.